All That Gorgeous Pitiless Song

Also by Rebecca Foust:

God, Seed (Tebot Bach Press: 2010), environmental poetry with art by Lorna Stevens.

Mom's Canoe (Texas Review Press: February 2009).

Dark Card (Texas Review Press: June 2008).

All That Gorgeous Pitiless Song

poetry by

Rebecca Foust

Many Mountains Moving Press
Philadelphia, Pennsylvania

Published by Many Mountains Moving Press.
http://mmmpress.org/

Many Mountains Moving Press is distributed by Small Press
Distribution, www.spdbooks.org/

Publishers Cataloging-in-Publication Data:
Foust, Rebecca
All That Gorgeous Pitiless Song / Rebecca Foust with a Foreword by
Steven Huff
—1st printing April 2010.
ISBN-13: 978-1-886976-24-5

Cover art: John F. Folinsbee (1898-1972), *Frozen River,* 1918, oil on
canvas, 16" x 20." Used by permission of the owners, from a private
collection in Pennsylvania. Copyright John F. Folinsbee Art Trust, all
rights reserved.

Design by Jeffrey Ethan Lee.
Copy editing by Brian Brodeur.

ACKNOWLEDGMENTS

Grateful acknowledgment is made to the following journals and chapbooks in which these poems have appeared or will appear:

Ars Medica for "The Peripheral Becomes Crucial." *Arts and Letters Journal* for "Father's Day Race." *Atlanta Review* for "Mom's Canoe," "Seeds of the Giant Sequoia" and "His First Death." *Café Review* for "Safari." *Canary* for "What Follows." *Cider Press Review* for "After the Hurricane" and "Herzog Out-Takes." *Clackamas Literary Review* for "Hope" and "Gray." *Cloudbank Literary Review* for "How Dad Got Caught." *Dogwood Poetry Review* for "A Kilogram of Salt" and "Neap Tide Wane." *Dos Passos Review* for "Altoona to Marin," here entitled "Altoona to Anywhere." *Flyway Journal* for "The Mountains Come Close," here entitled "Allegheny Mountain Bowl (Reprise)," and "Things Burn Down." *Iodine Journal* for "Books For The Blind." *Los Angeles Review* for "The Innocence Project." *Main Street Rag* for "The Dream." *Margie/The American Journal of Poetry* for "Backwoods," "Marrying Up" and "Apologies To My OB/GYN." *Marin Poetry Center 2007 Anthology* for "Windshadow." *Mudfish* for "Indian Pipe," "Purple Heart" and "No Longer Medusa." *Nimrod International Journal* for "How the Fish Feels" and "Sealed." *North American Review* for "Strip Mine" and "The Cormorant." *Off-Course Literary Journal* for "Sometimes the Mole Is Merely." *Poetry East* for "What's Happening." *Poetry Now* for "What Was Sacred." *Red Rock Review* for "Underneath," here entitled "Youngest Son," "Allegheny County Winter Day" and "The Bees Are Inside." *Spoon River Poetry Review* for "Crickets at Lakemont Park," "Pentimenti" and "The Well." *Texas Review* for "Archeological Record," "Once Was a River" and "Raystown River Trout." *The Cincinnati Review* for "What You Work For." *The Green Hills Literary Lantern* for "Origin." *The Hudson Review* for "From Function, Form." *The MacGuffin* for "American Dream," here entitled "California." *The Pedestal Magazine* for "Wild Swan." *The Sow's Ear Poetry Review* for "Family Story Told to Fourth Child." *The Woman's Review of Books* for "Water Burial."

Some of these poems appeared previously in *Dark Card* (Texas Review Press: June 2008), 2007 Robert Phillips Poetry Chapbook Prize, and *Mom's Canoe* (Texas Review Press: February 2009), 2008 Robert Phillips Poetry Chapbook Prize.

Some of the lines in "Allegheny Mountain Bowl" and *"Herzog* Out-takes" are from or inspired by Saul Bellow's *Herzog*.

Thanks to Mel Schorin for allowing me to use his line in "What Follows."

DEDICATION

To all the teachers who believed in me,
beginning with Miss Ruth Beck in the fifth grade at Baker School.

FOREWORD

Those of us who love poetry, who continue to turn to
it in the dark, not so much for solace but for the intimacy of
another's voice, know that we'll find a few new books each year
on the crowded street of poetry that we can sit down with,
and it will be like sitting with that odd stranger you meet with
whom, for reasons uncertain, you have an immediate and deep
communication and from which you will come away somehow
revivified. Maybe you've had similar busts or anxieties, or you
share a little pearl of bitterness or expectation. Who knows? But,
for me, Rebecca Foust's *All That Gorgeous Pitiless Song* is one of
those extraordinary strangers.

The opening poems are from a landscape of a coal and
railroad town, for all intents and purposes poisoned, and all too
familiar. We realize that something deeper than what poisoned
the water and the air has entered our bloodstream in a pandemic
way, from which our survival is anything but certain, but which
assumes a certain dire music:

> the same back porch weeping,
> the same husbands sleeping around,
> addiction, cancer, babies born wrong.
> The same siren nights pierced
> with stars seeping light, all that
> gorgeous, pitiless song.

The hopelessness of layoffs, mines dead, people flat broke, and,
as in "The Dream," disappointed dreams of adventure. But this
music is memory, and memory is music, and it has its inherent
beauty:

the sky's beautiful bruise.
These mountains calve memory from twilight,

some nuance you knew once like breath
comes back with the questions—why do mountains
come close when it rains....

Humanity as a whole is inseparable from it all; in fact, we're just the late end of geological history, "traced on slate, the mystery/of ancient fern or fish/or link to man." We're forced to remember that misery is no respecter of time or place, as noted in "Archeological Record," "Zeus is raping some girl/somewhere, you know that...."

And yet, hope is there, in fact, plenty of foolish hope (the best kind of hope, I always say); without it, this would be a lesser book. Dad going off to the dog races with his last forty bucks; mother starting the Sunday *New York Times* Crossword Puzzle the day she goes into hospice; and the willingness to love in a poisoned world, however it turns out: "you're my heart's phantom limb;/I don't know where I am."

It is indicative of the poet's skill that in the psychic nearness of events, the "you" persona of several of the poems could be almost anyone, possibly a dozen people you know:

your beloved canoe still lies on its side
split like your lip
where he kicked it,
the night you ran home to us
in your nightgown and only one shoe.

But there is also a refreshing demonstration of range. Foust can leave all that and include a series of odes to various species of tree, poems of pregnancy and the unborn. And, maybe most importantly, she can locate the sacred, which in one poem,

"What Was Sacred," is a bit of mere privacy and drawn curtains in a death room.

This is the kind of book that reminds me of why we cannot do without our poets. Not to give us hope on a plate by itself. But to give us a whole gallimaufry of trouble and worry and love, the music in which a foolish and hopeful dog will come to the door "where there's never been a bone." The whole gorgeous pitiless song.

—Steven Huff

CONTENTS

II

III

Altoona to Anywhere

Go ahead, aspire to transcend
your hardscrabble roots, bootstrap
the life you dream on,
escape the small-minded tyranny
of your mountain bound
coal mining town.

But when you've left it behind, you
may find it still there, in your dreams,
in your syntax, the smell of your hair,
its real smell under the shampoo.
Beware DNA. It will out or be outed,
and you'll find yourself back
where you started, back home, unable
to refute the logic of blood and bone,
you'll slip, and pick up the Velveeta
instead of the brie. It's inexorable.
Kansas one day will turn out to be Oz
and Oz Kansas,

with the same back porch weeping,
the same husbands sleeping around,
addiction, cancer, babies born wrong.
The same siren nights pierced
with stars seeping light, all that
gorgeous, pitiless song.

I

Allegheny Mountain Bowl

You can turn round and round and round and
always see mountains. Blue Knob, Wopsononock,
Brush, Davis and Lock. They usurp the sky
and conjure the seasons—summer's heavy
wet sails, stars slung low like lanterns,

lily-thronged ditches down in the cove.
Gashed-ember October, leaves falling like ash.
Winter's white bowl piles drift upon drift,
the air a thin gruel the men sip, waiting
for Blue Law noon. Their coats exhale wet wool

and wood smoke, their feet beat a work boot tattoo:
laid off, laid off, laid off—the mines mined out
and the Railroad dead, engines rusted to tracks.
Bitter cold at the root and bought too dear,
a hundred-year oak is two weeks' cordwood,

a doe is meat roped to the hood of your car.
Cinders and salt and snow turned black
and always the need to make rent. But have you seen
the trees' fierce diadems after the ice storms? And doesn't spring
finally come, skies fledged soft as new life,

fields drenched in dew? The lark in the morning,
thrushes at dusk; sometimes there are barn owls.
Look at Wopsy and Brush going dark,
the sky's beautiful bruise.
These mountains calve memory from twilight,

and some nuance you knew once like breath
comes back with the questions—why do mountains
come close when it rains, what line divides false
from true, in what precise place do the mountains
efface into sky—indigo, violet, then blue?

Strip Mine

A terrible, lunar beauty,
like leaves past withering.
When we run along the edges,
slag bits break loose and
roll down the wash
to the bottom,
pebbles round
as dark marbles,
two halves of ancient bivalve
face each other
in frozen contemplation,
the animating spark
buried in sediment
eons ago.

At the edge,
wild chicory adds blue
to the green and white tangle
of bindweed and Queen Anne's lace,
then, the shallow mine pit,
wide, rusty gash,
nakedness of rock
scoured of soil by the rains
since the miners packed up their rig
and left

this ledge with crumbling face
of limestone, gneiss, and shale.
Whole trays of layers separate
to reveal the delicate calligraphy
traced on slate, the mystery
of ancient fern or fish
or link to man.

Archeological Record

Scotch straight-up, thy neighbor's
wife and Sunday Church
—nobody's talking

but one white glove is lost.
What was said, and not. Gaps
outline the years laid down

in stone, but each wedged-in bit
is rocking. Dreams, cookbook
notes, the dress a mother wore

to a father's wake, or would
have worn—had she gone?
The pieces meet to make

a pot you haven't seen before,
the walls are half-effaced,
but Zeus is raping some girl

somewhere, you know that
much. It's all here—battle,
faun, flush of dawn, grapes

twined into leafy crowns,
each loved thing lost, sieved
with bitter salt and ash.

The Bees Are Inside

We played TV tag under the tree, Casey
and me, screaming, scrambling away
from the bees. He tagged me out once

under its leaves, then showed me his secret,
what he'd found on the tracks. He gave me
his best chunk of railroad glass, the size

of my fist; he gave me *The Hope Diamond.*
He had a face something fey, clear
as daylight in winter, too finely drawn.

How had he come from that stumbling line,
brawling and surly, dead-drunk by noon?
Not from his father those clear blue eyes,

not from his mother that hair like light—
Casey and kin were dawn and night, a bright
crystalline thing born out of darkness

and chaos. *Inbred,* they called him, and worse,
and sometimes he heard them. I saw
a cursed angel or changeling flung headlong from God

and then flung from a tree
we'd climbed a thousand times. It took
a purposeful, soaring fall,

the town whisper-buzz whispering like it had
for years, and we kids not meant to hear
the rest, all that was twisted and broken.

Eyes clear blue, hair like light, he said it
all through the night that he died.
The bees, he said, *the bees*
are inside. The bees are in my head.

Things Burn Down

My parents wouldn't come back for damask
napkins or oysters in frilly white shells.
If you understand, you won't have to ask

how Gramma knew linen—soiled, in the wash
she took in each week—or why she had to sell
baked goods in the street off "white trash damask,"

yesterday's newspaper. Papap hauled ash
or laid brick; he was skilled with a trowel
but there was no work, understand? Don't ask

what keeps a man from filling his flask
with what he'd divined from the wells he'd drilled
with his own hands, or why Dad's damask

was a gray square he hacked on to clear the ash
from his throat. Thick smoke from the paper mill
all day and night, understand? No one asked

in those days if that shit could kill you. As track
spread in congeries from the repair yards, fields
disappeared. Cinder and soot, more soot—damask

was *work* in that town. Mom found a dog lashed
to a tree, starved to bone. Too many mouths to feed,
do you understand that? She didn't ask

for much more than Sears Roebuck placemats
and babies that lived. What Dad loved was bells
and sirens, to watch things burn down. You ask

what would bring my dead folks back? I'd guess
garage sales, four-alarm fire bells, red squalls
of new babies, maybe a bratwurst and beer

served on an unfolded *Altoona Mirror.* Not damask,
not fingerbowls for Christ's sake. If you don't
get it by now, don't ask.

How Dad Got Caught

Mom's at the Raystown Dam asleep in the pop-up
cranked into its campsite where you think I am too
when you come back to the townhouse at dawn,
your sweat-slick palms, your *please, please
don't-tell-your-Moms*.

The morning is dark on the new redwood deck
divided from the freeway by a strip of green
it takes five minutes to mow. The new carpet
is still out-gassing its toxins under Mom's
pinchpleated drapes. When we moved,

you kept saying it felt great not being in hock,
not having to pull weeds, take down screens,
put up strings of lights—Mom rolled the last knot
between finger and thumb, bit off the thread.
I thought about the red and green glow of bulbs

under new snow, and our old back porch rambling
with summer's wild roses. How at night the house
sometimes got too close, all camphor and dust
and heat like a wall, but outside, the back lawn strewn
with fireflies, cool air, and the dew line drawn.

The Dream

My father dreamed all his life of a cruise:
sleek bandbox staterooms, turquoise water, hot light,
hints of unbound sex, indolent spice-scented air,
platters piled high with pineappled shrimp.

He wore the right shoes when shopping at Kmart,
bright white, and Panama hats and leisure suits
in tropical hues. We all laughed, but we stopped after
he got sick, shivered, had night sweats, lost hair,

was drawn to bone in the stiff polyesters, head
magic-marker-mapped. He tried to hang on
but lost ground, returned in his dreams to shivering
at Bastogne, shoveling lime into Kaufering cattle cars,

to the year that taught him lust for every fresh-picked
ear of corn, red marigolds in a white plastic pot,
a salmon-pink blazer, life intact in the precise way
each fork was placed. When he got home

and felt safe, he began to dream big: exotic islands
under plumbago skies, winters with warm,
moist air, heaped platters everywhere and no trains
anywhere in sight. Until he got sick and learned

again how to long just for anything not broken,
and his dream-cruise diffused into the mere idea
of a voyage, or one someone else took, and then
he began to dream in earnest:

Light. Warmth. Food. Breath. Until he dreamed
himself dreaming a dream, then nothing.

Water Burial

I watched the cure flense him,
unwinding blubber and flesh
from the great, floating carcass

of body, turning it in water,
unpeeling like paring an apple
and winding it back up

onto the dark spindle. I saw
the cure grapple-hook
his spirit to strip it in spirals

from where it had once
adhered to his heart.
I saw him reduced

to a jawbone a man
could stand up
and walk through.

Moon on Snow

The kitten mews again.
And again. We fall all over
each other to push

the morphine pump
button, can't stand another
second of that sound.

We'd gotten used
to stick arms and legs,
his slipping toupee

that looked like his dog
who died first, last week,
but what's in that bed

barely looks human,
carbuncle face, water-balloon
hands. When we cut

off the tourniquet socks
the skin's black, like the skin
around his groin.

We check the catheter
in compulsive catechism.
Empty two days now,

the body's shutting down.
Send back the food that not
even the living can eat.

My brother cries
in the bathroom in case Dad
can hear him.

We collapse in a circle
around his bed. He gave up
knowing us yesterday,

gave up talking last night,
so afraid of the shelling
he wailed like a child.

His WWII souvenir bayonet
hung high on the pegboard
with old oiled tools

over the workbench
where he taught me sand block,
miter box and plane.

It was my turn to spend the night
in the orange plastic recliner that
did not recline, my turn

to get up to press the button
on cue with the mewing
in the light-blinking dark,

my turn for shame in my wish
the mewing would stop,
my turn to know

the time when his time came.
Outside, a few soundless flakes,
silver moon on snow.

Mineshaft Memory

You patted my hand
while you died,
helped birth
my three babies,
stood for my wedding,
paid mill money
for college,

made sugar-and-butter toast
to cure me
of my first,
faithless boyfriends,
brewed hot
cambric tea
in frozen
school dawns,

pointed to what
you'd appliquéd
on my baby sweater
and painted
on my plywood dresser,
touched finger
to lips and said
the word *lamb*.

You're my soul's
phantom limb;
I don't know now
where I am.

Books for the Blind

Blind from diabetes,
Gramma sat in her
bentwood rocker
and tapped out her hours
on the front stoop.
She could get around
well enough to use
the bathroom,
pull on her hairnet
and support hose,
make coffee and fry up
scrapple for breakfast,
then move to the porch
to sip wind and weather,
drink liquid birdsong
and wait. Mom mail-ordered
the books each week from
The Library of Congress,
lugged them across the
cow-grated, slick-slatted
bridge, up the dirt path past
the old hand plough
subsiding to rust, to
the leaning white farmhouse
in need of new paint.
Each book was the
weight of a small child
or *damn greyhound bus*
and as clumsy to carry,
hitched up on Mom's hip.
Thick, flat plastic square,

like the hard-sided case
you might pack a bomb in,
all done up with buckles
and seatbelt-size straps.
Gramma's fingers frantic,
fumbling at the catch.

Family Story Told to Fourth Child

Mom talked about how when the x-ray
used in those days before ultrasound
confirmed she was pregnant again, and
with her second set of twins, she buttoned up
her best going-out dress, wondering
what are those dark spots, adjusted her hat
and left. Weeks later she realized what they
were: tears for the long years before
the long years ahead—diapers, glass bottles,
nights without sleep, no help with wailing kids
but from more wailing kids.
             She wept like she lived,
and when the drops bloomed on the gray wool
of her dress, she looked up at the changing room
ceiling, expecting to find rain.

Backwoods

You'd go back to him, then,
your swaggering full-bird
second husband, fragged in Korea
and now hunkered down
here in this backwater?

How could you,
after he blackened
your eye,
dumb-bitched you
and wrecked your canoe?

You escaped from that place once,
his cottage collapsed
on the banks of that dirty, dredged ditch
he calls a river. All you needed was a car
where you could sleep, keep your things.

Yes, you're alone now that we kids
are all grown. But would you
really go back
to that tarpaper shack
squatting in bottles and weeds,

where your beloved canoe still lies on its side
split like your lip
where he kicked it,
the night you ran home to us
in your nightgown and only one shoe.

Purple Heart

Every death has its interest, its spike
of tragedy or farce. Take yours,
face down in the bathroom four days,
naked except for black socks,

inhalant in hand, door locked
in the cottage where you'd lived alone
for three years after Mom left.
You didn't even feel your broken nose,

Forensics said, able to read
the dried blood pattern-spray
and the tea leaves of what you'd
left in the toilet; there was the

enlarged matter of your heart,
your Agent Orange-burned lungs.
Did it give you pause, before you
gasp-gagged and fell forward?

You blamed the *niggers* and *gooks*
for stealing your country, but for
forty years you couldn't breathe
well enough to walk to the bathroom

without your inhaler, and three
tours in Korea cost you your wife
and sad, cutter daughter. You
were passed over five times

for promotion and in the end died
this way, heart-attacked, straining
your shrapneled bowels.
The calamitous stink of you,

face-down alone for four days
before strangers kicked in the door.

Once Was a River

His cottage down in the Cove
—mildew and wild roses,
thick vines choking

everything, outhouse,
grid bridge over sludge,
what once was a river.

The walkway exhumed
brick by brick from
sewage-soaked mud,

oak and elm limbs
locked up overhead,
old bottles

stuck into cinderblocks
under the joists. The gin
dumped down the drain

the day he woke up sober
by accident and saw
a future spent

behind rusted screens,
wrist-clamped to sad wicker,
rocking his terrible thirst.

Indian Pipe

Wild woodland flower found
pushing through humus
in moss and fern fen. Rare,
lucent and cave-dwelling fish.

Pale, cool glow, something
hothouse or orchid or mushroom
that melts at touch
or in too much sun—your skin

is like that, thin membrane over
blue pulse, architecture of small bones
that build the body that
fostered five children.

I'm twice your size now, unrolling
blinds against the light, wrapping
you up in your blue flannel bathrobe,
so little of you left.

What Was Sacred

It took a long time for your body
to grow cold in the dawn
of your dying, but the AC did its work
and I waited, holding your hand
until I was sure you were gone.

They left us alone for the time that it took,
and the curtains were drawn for respect.
Afterwards, I stayed in your room
to hold hands
with the mail-order chaplain

and watch the sun heave its blaze up
over Brush Mountain, scatter
the gray embers of day.

Gray

was the color of your hair, soft gunmetal glint
like the mill steel of cord-stacked girders
at the railroad repair yard, gray like
the library façade, limestone so soot-soaked
it looked like metal, gray like
the man's hankie you wore to school, a bandit,
running past the mills where your father

learned to lay brick and set stone. He taught
you how to canoe the river, turn handsprings
and skate backwards better than any boy.
You watched him diminish and dim into
his rocking chair, crying just once, when
that fool kid killed the hawk that had cut
dips and arcs into his twilights.

Your face suffused with the glow of snow bank
bonfires, you skated backwards holding my hands
so I could skate forwards. We dipped and arced,
etched the dark ice. You taught me how to feather
a stroke, swim the width of the warm, brown river.
But it got you too; the lung sickness furnace
reduced you to prime number purity.

I watched you diminish and dim, sunset
leaching into sepia night; twilight
caught in the net of your long, gray lashes.
Your feet, fingertips, then your sweet face
drained. All of you gone
but these few bits of bone
left sifting your body, your ashes.

Mom's Canoe

Do you remember your old canoe?
Wooden, wide-bellied, tapered ends
made to slip through tight river bends
swiftly, like shadow.
Hull hollow-ribbed, wing of bird,
skimming the water more glider than boat,
ponderous in portage, weightless afloat.
Frail origami, vessel of air,
wide shallow saucer suspended where
shallows met shadows near the old dam.
Remember how it glowed like summer honey,
rubbed with beeswax and turpentine
against leaks, cracks, weather and time?
All your housekeeping went into that canoe,
riding bow lifted, arced up like flight,
you j-stroking, side-slipping, eddying out.
Frugal with movement, all without effort,
like you walked and ran. I still see you
rising from water to sky,
paddle held high,
river drops limning its edge.
Brown diamonds catch the light
as you lift, then dip.
Parting the current, you slip
through the evening shadows.
You, birdsong, watersong, slanting light,
following a river bend, swallowed from sight.

Origin

I was still pigtailed and pinafored in the fifth grade
while cool girls were rolling their eyes, their hair,
and their waistbands to shorten their skirts.
I hoped to impress them with my Science Project
(which goes to show how clued-in I was then
to social nuance). I filled a beaker

with water, corked it, and pumped in some air.
A little cloud formed, feathery and delicate,
and I felt powerful, like God
in awe of my own creation. Until it exploded,
and a shard just missed some short-skirted eye.
I cried when I was banished

to the dark cloakroom, and I felt abject like Lucifer,
just wanting to be in with the archangel
in-crowd. *What on God's earth
were you thinking,* Mom asked me later,
*pumping air into a bottle sealed
with no valve?* The truth is

that I was too mesmerized by my miracle to see
past the cloud. The truth is that even when
I was a part of things I felt apart
from things, that while I cried those tears
in my dark closet exile, I also felt free—
I felt an icicle splinter of glee.

Allegheny County Winter Day

Ads for "Farmettes!"
in the morning edition
of the *Altoona Mirror*,
a single black buggy

sifts snow down
the back roads
past green-roofed houses
built solid with field stone,

outlasting the people
willing to live there.
Square white barns
in sparkle-stick fields

set at right angles
to the dark tree line.
Last night's snowfall
sunk under noon sun,

dull shine of whipped
egg whites. The old
Boyer Candy plant
has gone dark.

Day slants towards
dusk, the sound not
of birdsong but wings,
lifting up all at once

for late winter migration.
The six o'clock train
whistle bends its long,
hollow plaint round

the Horseshoe Curve
(the former eighth
wonder of the
engineered world).

Everyone's going
or gone. Sunset bleeds
through bare boughs;
snow hollows go blue.

II

Wild Swan

What I knit at night
unravels each dawn,
yarn slipping like smoke
from the day's
bright needles. A prince
once was a boy,
a swan, my autistic son.

It burns, it burns,
his garment of nettle,
his singlet of stars.
The night cries
are feral and awful;
my hours are
cloistered with wool.

I make the knots faster,
knowing what
morning will bring:
at his lips, one white
crescent pinfeather, fluttering,
under the counterpane
his shining wing.

What You Work For

Heft and hank of rope, halyard
clank of ringing chain

dragged link by gunnel-clunking link
and hand-over-hand hauled in

until at end, sudden greased release
of anchor weight

and you fall back, stunned by what
your dragging work has yoked

you to. Has brought
aboard to share your boat.

Pentimenti

Young, she dreamed of things she wanted
to have for her own, like the thick rugs
she clotheslined and beat each week,
the silver embossed with her own family crest,
porcelain fine enough
to let light through,
a garden instead of a driveway.

When she got them, the rugs glowed
like cathedral glass and swallowed her
bare feet in plush. Rooms shimmered
and hung in the air. Clavicle teacups,
cutlery weighted to fit her hand
like a weapon. It felt like entitlement
until she began to hear night sounds,

whispers, sobs, ululations in the pipes
of a house drinking its village-ration
of water each week and still so dry.
Time rubbed away the faces of things,
showed brushstrokes beneath. When she
looked through the keyhole Tabriz,
they sat in long rows, each child weaver

tied to a loom. She touched her tongue
to the Meissen's worn spot and tasted
its translucent secret, a soupçon
of human bone. The engraved spoon
dropped from her hand, branded her
with silver, white-hot and mined
from men's veins, etched in elaborate
fretwork in the dark, deep underground.

Marrying Up

Some things were easy, like writing the check
for her last student loan and learning to open
the mailbox without fear
of the bills that would be there
and bailing out her dad the year the IRS
made good on its threat to garnish his wages.

It's been great to have health insurance;
going to the dentist for an abscess sucks
but beats the alternative, cheap-whiskey
anodyne tucked like chew in the cheek
until the tooth dies or is pliered out. She's
mastered driving a car the size of a room

or her first apartment; perhaps soon she
can handle the Hummer. She no longer
questions the necklace or ring that cost more
than the house her dad couldn't keep, is able
to sleep on the beach at Club Med
where the guy with the machine gun guards

lounge chairs. She takes her oblivion where
she can find it: fundraiser wine, coffee mug
gin, heroin, maybe turning Republican.
At least then she could carry a gun just for fun,
or to blow out her brains next time
she sees one of those necklace's gumball-size

pearls plucked out by the *Ama* who dive down
on one breath. Who sometimes drown.

Safari

Our family is going to Africa.
We've been doing the pill regimen
for months, very stressful.
We've engaged a fifteen-person entourage
for our family of five;
Dad's bought a camera the size
of a handheld grenade launcher,
and we duck and cover
when he brings it to dinner.
I've planned my wardrobe, outsize
sunglasses and visors
that won't wreck my hair.

It's "real Safari" conditions, so
we'll camp in tents of breathable canvas
pitched by Abercrombie & Fitch.
There will be cool, moving air
in the steaming savannahs,
and morning coffee served by the same
hands that picked the beans
and brewed the cup,
and will wash it up afterwards.
At night we will dine on spit-roasted
zebra, Cape buffalo, antelope, gnu.

And if one of the kids gets malaria,
as tourists sometimes do,
we'll be outraged,
demand refunds and sue
the whole country: its dirt, its trees,
its poignant expanses and horizonless skies
of implacable azure,
its impartial flies.

Too Soon

It's not your fault, my doctor says,
that my cervix is incompetent
a thousand ways, or that the DES
prescribed for mom's miscarriages
merely deferred them to me.

Now here I lie on my left side,
mandolin belly for the moment alive
with my restless son; my hands
make a cradle, rocking him early to sleep.

My labor heaves up in waves
like the moon-crazed tide; it raves
like the tide-crazed moon,
rising and rising too soon, too soon.

I can't get my breath—my gown's
soaked with milk, all spilt.
The doctor looks young and afraid.
The nurse asks me, *Have you ever prayed?*

His First Death

He died when he was born
for ten or more seconds
while I drew in three long breaths.
The hand pump hissed
and his face was dusk. I dreamed
the dreams mothers dream
for their first sons—kick and suck,
pupils that tighten in sunlight,
stand, walk and run. Act-out
and talk-back, eye met by eye,
roll in wet grass. Three beats
passed. His Dixie-cup chest
inflated, then crumpled. I drew in
and released my own great
useless lung loads, each profligate breath.

Apologies to My OB/GYN

Sorry that my boy birthed himself
too early, took up so much room
in your prenatal nursery
with his two pounds, two ounces
and did not oblige your nurses
with easy veins.

Sorry we were such pains in your ass,
asking you to answer our night calls like that,
and that he did everything so backwards:
lost weight, gained fluid,
blew up like a human balloon
then shriveled.

Sorry about how he defied your prognoses,
skyrocketed premiums, weighted the costs
in your cost-benefit analyses,
skewed bell-curve predictions
into one long, straight line.
Sorry he took so much of your time

being so determined to live. He spent
today saving hopeless-case nymph moths
trapped in the porch light, one matrix-dot
at a time. Now he's asleep, blue wingbeat
pulse fluttering his left temple—there,
there again. Just like it did then.

The Cormorant

"[Satan] flew, and on the Tree of Life...
Sat like a Cormorant...."
—*Paradise Lost,* Book IV, lines 194-96

The four-chambered heart and wings
somehow transcend his reptilian brain
and come with dusty black feathers

that fray the frockcoat of this dour,
penurious parson. An oddly dense
puddle of shadow inking the float,

he does not deign even one glance
in our direction. We dog-paddle close,
but he waits until we touch wood

to unfold awkward, creaking wing,
splash down on water, upend, dive
and, sleek as a snake, disappear,

no ripple or wake. We climb up, cold and late. The sun
in decline has turned the lake red. It's already starting to burn.

What Follows

If a tree falls and no one hears,
then it didn't fall, you'd say, but
I say the tree would know it fell,

and so would the hive-world
that had hummed and teemed
in its leaves. And the flowers

would know, each sticky stamen
barren of pollen. *Okay,* you say,
then think of a rock

that fell, and I didn't hear it. Well,
I see earth's new crater, blades
of grass bent, dust disturbed;

each perturbed molecule knows
that rock fell. *Okay, so it happened,*
you'd say, *but not for me, not*

my reality if I didn't hear or see it.
But I say my reality is one web
with strands that go everywhere

so that mine waste, washed down
a river, wafts its effluent plume
through estuary and ocean

connecting endless land to endless
land that I walk through, the air
I breathe in. I never even licked

that apple, but my heel still
is stung. With original sin,
it only begins.

A Kilogram of Salt

Elfriede Rinkel was 84 the year she was outed as a Ravensbrück Guard
and deported to Germany. This rickety old lady lived in San Francisco

for three decades married to a German-born Jew, both scarred, it was thought,
by the Holocaust. They held hands in the street, waltzed past the windows

of their walk-up at night, made plans to be buried in side-by-side graves.
Those chevra kadisha workers knew a thing or two about salt, how much

it takes to purify the body after death, how much you must eat at table
with a friend to begin to know him, how much you must yourself eat

to make amends. The Feds say that she worked at that death camp for most
of a year, that she marched women under attack dogs to the worksites,

drove them half-dead and dazed. She said she didn't see the newborns
drowned in tin pails while their mothers were made to watch. She said

she worked there for less than a year, just a girl when she answered the ad
and was told to guard or be guarded, that she fled when she could.

The Nazi hunters' message was brittle and clear. None of it matters, not
how naïve you were or were not, not your fear, not what was chosen

or chance, not how you hoped to advance or atone. What matters: eight million
dead and you either part of the machine or ground up in its gears.

But the truth is not like that, not whole and clear. Truth is more fragmented,
shards that fall in the night, daggers, stars, diamonds and razors—

in truth you can eat a dead ocean of salt with yourself and still not know
which version is right, what really happened or why. The mind is adept

at shoring things up. Take Fred Rinkel, who trained as a tenor in Berlin,
then escaped to this country, found work singing Puccini

and serving spaghetti to tourists who called him *Vinny* or *Sal*. He married
Elfriede, whose past was *my business,* she said. They waltzed

and held hands, paid their respects at the cemetery. He died the year before
she paid the bills, turned off the pilot light and phone, said no

goodbyes to anyone, not even her brother living in Oakland, and held out
her baton-thin, purse-dangling arm to be led to the plane.

How the Fish Feels

hooked, jerked up from all
it knew; fluid, muted milieu
before bright bite of metal.

Gills burned, drowned in air,
under slanted blade, afraid
as rainbow armor scales away.

Laid wide open, butterflied,
broken-booked, spine revealed,
entrails tangled overboard.

Gutted, cut to bone
past pain or thought or
twitch of brain.

Herzog Out-takes

The need to clarify, to make amends.
He heard the crow in the morning;
its harsh cry was delicious. He heard
the thrushes at dusk. At night
there were barn owls. *If I am out
of my mind,* he thought, *it's all right
with me.* Absurdly tranquil, radiant.

The need to explain, to have it out,
to justify, to put into perspective
the unconscious frankness of a man
deeply preoccupied—
he suspected it might be a symptom
of disintegration. His clinical picture,
depressive. The Rorschach recalled

the teeth on the dogfish at the City
Aquarium, its sad brown eyes and
expression of betrayal. His ex-wife's
skin was subtle, animate and white.
The sun in its cold bottle, thick, opaque,
frozen under the lake; wide open eyes
never sleep. Snow in drift
and more drift. A fish that weeps.

Father's Day Race

The boat had no hull; it was a wing
fired in porcelain, glass and steel
skimming the waves and our girl gone

with you to let out the mainsail. The win
was what mattered, speed and style.
The boat had no hull, just a wing

so that waves slipped past like Teflon,
your mast tall and great sail full,
skimming the waves, our girl keen

on your scent. You could not begin
to take enough care, so you took none at all.
The boat had no hull but a wing

for speed and style, no ballast or concern
for safe—just cut wake, caressed foil.
It skimmed the waves, our girl gone

over the side to rescue the rigging. No will
now, no mast, no cumbersome life vest.
The boat had nothing under its wing;
it skimmed the waves, and our girl was gone.

He Never Lies

not because he won't
or doesn't know better,
or how, he just can't.
I imagine him telling
too much of a truth,
or hell-bent on one
of his endless, spiraling,
descending dissents.

I fear he'll be over blunt
or otherwise by accident
draw their attention,
annoyance, their rage.
How far might they
go to assuage discomfort
with difference?
I imagine him drugged
or locked down on a ward.
In my nightmare
he's caged.

Sealed

There's a
certain pain
that cauterizes
any stump
or what remains,

solders seams
so seamlessly,
so thoroughly
embalms

that nothing
can leak out
or in—

no break
or blow
or jolt of joy,
nor ache
of phantom limb.

Seeds of the Giant Sequoia

come cone-born, encased
in diamond-hard coats;
something secreted
encrypts them against
climate and time,
lets them wait out
the cold-ground
generations of winters
for that lightning-crack,
thunderbolt trunk-split of fire
that will fissure them to life.

Dull glitter of years
layering down. But when
the firestorm comes,
the ground melts and boils
like stew, swelling each seed
from germ to koan,
seeking meaning
from rain, memory
from pain, how it feels
to feel anything.

III

What's Happening

is what happens
to quince
when it renounces
sap-sleep
for bloom

to sun, nudging
off noon

to fledgling, fallen
into flight

to pupa when
it ruptures
cocoon

to seed when
it cracks
awake

to Bald Mountain's
terrible thirst
fog-slaked
in June.

The Innocence Project

For Wilton Dedge

The State argued its case four times in four trial courts
in front of a judge who hand-picked the four juries.

When three of them hung, the State still pressed its case
to have you strung up too, kept calling for juries.

The fourth one convicted you: battery and rape
based on one hair and a jail snitch's perjuries.

When he cracked on the stand and recanted, the DA
still had the hair, displayed to the jurors,

evidence that Justice was not blind but could see
that blond-matches-blond, perfect logic for juries.

You were only nineteen. For the next twenty years
you sat on death row, the hair stowed in cold storage

until science caught up, showed DNA cannot lie
like men can, or err, or spin stories for juries.

When the swab yielded sperm from four men, but not yours,
the State freed you at last, regretted your injuries

but did not redress them. You were left on your own
twenty years in arrears, beleaguered by furies.

Still, you are exonerated, not a felon, free to vote
and to fight and to tell your stories

to school audiences like this one, who at least
give a shit, think it not fair and that you are brave

for continuing to suck air and not killing
someone, the judge, or your entire fourth jury.

Exact and aloof as math, this DNA proof—
God's own signature, not subject to forgeries.

California

Maybe it was the way
she swayed
that pond-lily, heavy-headed
filament-legged sway,
the clotted-cream white throat
of the one riotous bloom,
her blue-veined petal skin
and bright pollen hair;

maybe, how she'd bend
and turn to show
every curve at once
—lip and lash, flat
wide bowl of hip, its taper
and swell, or maybe
it was the smell of bracken;

the smell of bracken,
and further in of tide
and at the heart
that absinthe hint,
fleeting subtle sweet
allelopathic rot of root
and slow decay.

Hope

I.
Mom starting the
Times Sunday crossword
her first day in hospice

II.
The measuring tape
my 12-year-old son
keeps in his bedroom

III.
Papap buying corn on the cob
at the farm stand,
his teeth in his pocket

IV.
Anything with feathers
that will against all odds
go aloft

V.
Bill the dog at the door
where there's never
been a bone

VI.
Dad going for
the dog track trifecta
with his last forty bucks

VII.
Ms. Stone smiling
when we sat down
for our parent conference

VIII.
Heart carbonation;
maybe it's not
an infarction

IX.
The exact shade of pink-red
of the bare-branched
flowering quince

X.
Spring after nuclear
winter, and nucleus—
nucleus of anything

No Longer Medusa

When I had you, daughter, I gave birth
to my mirror,
the chink in my armor.
Once, I turned men to adamantine
with a glance, dove from cliffs
into dark quarries, swung grapevines
over ravines, rode arcs of tall birch trees
into the ground. Now I am alive
all night with fear for you, undone
by your sweet, milky breath,
the bobcat tufts on your ears,
your pink ribbon gums.
You freeze my heart to stone
when I measure your foot with my thumb.

Youngest Son

Beneath days as blank and calm
as a kettle pond dawn swarm
tadpoles, minnows, perch,

barbed hooks, snarled lines,
snakes, algae strands thick
as ropes to pull you down,

filaments tethering lily stars
that from above seem free to skim,
milky writhe of swimmers' legs,

mossed undersides of floats,
the surprising truth of sailboat keels,
their iceberg depth.

The Peripheral Becomes Crucial

in ways we'd never have guessed, like when
they unwound the crocodile-mummy shroud
focusing on what was within,

casting aside as trash the papyri
which, when kicked, unscrolled to reveal
what Sappho wrote.

Sometimes more is inscribed
in the chemical signature of mud
than in the Sanskrit writ on the pot.

My son is gentler with moths
than people ever were with him,
and he chooses truth like breath.

He sets out cutlery backwards at table,
every time; he shaman-finds the bird point
flint, the fish spine, the speckled egg.

We watch as the linen-strip, tight-wrap coil
of that Gordian-knot neck-throttled curse,
that gene-encrypted, linked-chain curse,

that DES-taken-by-grandmother curse,
that fumble-finger-fool-doctor-shaped curse,
unravels with his years, unwinds, unfolds,

lets loop out in vast uncoiling spirals
whole archives of text, found worlds.

Sometimes the Mole Is Merely

Sometimes they happen—bombs
blow up school buses, a son's shyness
is autism, the mole is more than a mole,
a teenager mistakes the brake for the gas

and that sound like a recycle truck drop-gate
where no truck should be and you run, you run
outside and see in the back wall of the garage
the cartoon-cutout shape the size of a car,
but the color of sky.

And when you stop and look through,
the car lolls on its back like a beetle, dazed
and still. Except that wheels still spin slowly
and inside, upside down, slowly swing

two freighted baskets of husband and son
suspended in seatbelts
that unbuckle to release them
in heaps; but this time, thank God,

heaps that move, unfold, extend,
crawl out flattened window frames,
stand up and walk out,
shivering off shards.

The Well

A boy, straight, clear-eyed, grown into a man and loved
by a woman, my could-have-been son.

Urdu. Persian. Arabic—tongues ululate for the beloved
dreamed of, then lost, a could-have-been son?

Replenish the vessel of grief with longing for what never
was, and also what is: man-child

with planets for eyes, stars drowned in underground lakes
for eyes, no ladder down to reach what

could have been, son, no ladder to pull you out. Children
are born, and grow old with one another

while their parents grow older and die. This is the natural
order of things, but who, my gone-down-the-well son,

who will grow old with you? Remind you to eat? Haul you
up from the night terrors

that sometimes still swallow you whole? Who will love you,
and whom, whom

will you love? I tear my clothes, gash my face with sharp stones,
wander in traffic, lay my head down

on the warm, thrumming rail. I offer my life, but God will
not haggle. My orbit decays, and you

will be left alone with everything that could have been, son,
not made for this world. But since

Foust means *fist* and Rebecca *most faithful,* I'm bound
to divine a way back, to find

some fissure in God's own mind, maybe the same one
you fell through into baffled darkness.

We'll find the way out. Not up, trailing long braided ribbons
of bubbles, but down. Slung down

like stones. We'll find it together, the lost, freshet mouth
of the aquifer, the one that sings of the sea.

After the Hurricane

Nature went crazy after Hurricane Bob.
Salt-shocked leaves flamed red in July

against sky preternaturally blue. Pogies flew
then rained silver onto the beach,

bees grew confused and swarmed in the sea.
Marsh murmur hushed

in nights without light or sound, thick with black
but for Perseids and fireflies.

When the well failed, we forgot to be careful
and clean, we bathed with the salt

and sand in our hair, we went down
after dark to swim in a bay

swollen with tide, moonskimmed,
glittering green fire—

phosphorescent plankton—and the stars
streaked from the sky and were drowned.

Windshadow

It's quiet here in the windshadow, hills
and mountains of the island of you
humped up and dark in the dusky dawn
light of this room. The sun will
continue to come and continue to fill
the room until the shades must be drawn
against the blank flush and heat of afternoon.

I remember when the dawns and nights
were lush with windy light and rush and press
that glittered and crackled and boomed the sail.
It's quiet here now on the leeward side.
I can pull in the sheet, tack close to shore,
follow your contour,
your warm curve of landscape, and sleep.

Neap Tide Wane

I thought it would wane with my waning years,
but my moon blood rose
clotted and dark like blue-black earth
spaded over in spring after rain.
Not the change I expected,
I rejected its excess, its feral tang
and red-mouthed insistence
that I believe what I cannot conceive,
a child, new love, perhaps an idea.

But I have heard the exact tick of the tide-clock
and know the cost of each crimson bloom;
I know the blood that monthly makes its ebb
takes more than moon renews. Core tissue
sloughs, bones honeycomb like coral.
I lessen, lose mass and soon

I'll be dry and light, clean, bled white
as any beach-wrecked bit of bleached bone,
floated like a whisper, or a wish. A husk.

The Quarry

We got there by following
the old railroad grade,
tracks still glinting under leaf-mold,
curving away through green tunnels
of old trees; low branches swept us
laughing into the truck bed.

We broke through the woods
into the clear shock of light
and rocks scraped clean.
Mineshaft walls made a beaker
of stone holding an icy sluice
so deep that blue met black
in the center. No one had
touched bottom, ever, nor
seen the drowned gear
and *maybe miners,* hands frozen
to rigs and floating hair.

We shucked our clothes, spread
towels on the limestone ledge
Mardi-Grased with broken glass,
Queen Anne's lace, and blue-eyed
grass. We soaked in the heat,
air heavy with fat, lolling bees,
blackberries steeped into wine.
Every year some fool fell
from the rocks, but we climbed
the highest cliff and looked down
to where the chokecherry soaked
its roots, Jesus bugs danced a tarantella,
and mayflies splurged their single day.

Crickets at Lakemont Park

The crickets are sounding a catastrophe
outside my window, reminding me
of the painted tin clickers whose tongues

we'd arc and release, consolation prizes
for the perennially rigged ring toss,
that huge stuffed orangutan getting more

moth-eaten every year, smell of sweat
and hot axle grease, gear eating gear when
the paint-peeling rolly coaster creaked

its way up and plunged past the carousel,
the real crickets' jig-chorus racket
in the long-limbed grass where we spread

our thin blanket. Then the carnival light
and crackle would fade, then I'd arc
and release again and again. Your hands,
your tongue, the cricket-sung, mown-grass dark.

Raystown River Trout

It took my hook like kite-caught wind.
I had to fight to reel it in, to net
its taut dense-bodied surge, heft
and heave of oiled writhe.

I knew about the upstream mine,
uncapped and seeping mercury, so I
wore gloves to hold the fish no fool
would eat and waited for the mystery

and passion. But there was no rainbow,
rainbow, rainbow, no communion
with Christ's flesh. Just this prism
flash gone gray and my sick wish

I'd never caught it. I wished I'd cut
the line before the glitter got away.

November

Gray day
upon day
before snow,
old tintype
sepia tones

muted so
that color's
an incident,
a jewel
that glows.

Sunset caught
roseate in
each web
of branches;

bittersweet
wearing motley
beside the
back roads.

The signal's
an exotic,
daubed parrot
or harlot—

emerald. Burnt
gold. Then
throat-caught
scarlet.

From Function, Form

On the bus to Salinas, sectioned fields
plumed with blue sprinkler arcs.
A distant tractor trailed dust in rows

like Log Cabin quilt bars, alternating
wine, green and gray, like the earth
in its seasons. The quilt was Amish,

stitched-in-the-ditch, twelve dips per inch,
the hair-thin sharp rocking through cotton
in a lullaby rhythm, ten thousand stitches

in long, straight rows. In its sea of mute
color one bar was scarlet, a spark-caught
flame, and the wide gray borders

were a riot of quilted texture—hyacinth
curlicues, looping patterns called
Clamshell or Wave. I think of her,

three states away from any ocean, locked
in long days patterned on piety, a woman
slipping in fancywork to break up the plain.

But when it turned in the distance,
the tractor blazed red, its back wheels
tracing great, slow arcs in a sea

of dust to begin the next row. Not some
whimsy or homespun rebellion,
but a faithful rendering. What she saw.

Allegheny Mountain Bowl (Reprise)

Now she can see how the dull edge of a scaler
(when all you wanted was a few hours fishing)
could bring on a curse, how butchering a deer
could be an elegy for life as it used to be,
simple, clear, in its way abundant—when a man's
family was hungry, he got them some meat.

And say it's ten below zero, skies gray so long you
forget what blue looks like, and you can't find a job.
Why not wait for the V.A. to open, your breath
hanging white sheets in the air? Easy for a girl
reading *Ivanhoe* to natter on about diademed branches
and fledged clouds over fields still frozen like iron

in April; she wasn't splitting the furnace wood; she
didn't have to dredge the well the summer it went
foul. A grain sack held four onyx-tipped deer legs,
each one sawed clean at the knee. Call it a prank,
hillbilly road rage. Here, the water doesn't taste of
bad meat or metal, but sometimes at night it glows,

warmed by a faint but distinct radioactive plume,
the fruit perfect, but babies born blighted beyond
ken or control. Here, she spits her curses at traffic
and weeps when the oven shorts out the third time
in a week. The underground cistern is dry. Her arms
bloom pansies, blue, purple, brown. Winter's chill

steals into her bones. She longs for home, rusted rails
going nowhere, fields frozen in furrow and rut,
mothwing tracks paired to the saltlick, tall hedgerow
snowdrifts in the high winter. Skies in a rainbow
of yellows, blues bleeding to violets, mine pits
that open their mouths to speak in precise fossils,

where boys fly from precipice rocks and dark trees,
and sometimes survive. Spring breaks her green vow
and fades into fall. The whole falls apart, but still
each bit glitters, glitters, brown diamonds on water.
Look outside and you'll see it, the barest nuance
of season, one backlit leaf against a dark bough.

ABOUT THE AUTHOR

Rebecca Foust won the
2008 MMM Press
Poetry Book Prize for
*All That Gorgeous Pitiless
Song*. Her other books
include *God, Seed*
(forthcoming from
Tebot Bach Press: 2010),
environmental poetry
with art by Lorna
Stevens, and two
chapbooks, *Mom's Canoe*
and *Dark Card* (Robert
Phillips Poetry Chap-
book Prizes, 2007 and
2008). Foust received
her MFA from Warren
Wilson College in 2010.